# high diary it's me, hannah

hannah jane

BookLeaf Publishing

India | USA | UK

Presentation by *BookLeaf Publishing*

Web: www.bookleafpub.com

E-mail: info@bookleafpub.com

ISBN: 9789363317260

First edition 2024

*to the people i love, you set my soul on fire*

# PREFACE

if you know me personally, no you do not. this is so raw and vulnerable and wild. probably a little destructive as well, but i've learned life is meant to be blown up and shifted and seized. i can see so clearly the picture in my mind where the story started in london in the summer of 2020 where i started to grow a love for taylor swift and a love for myself. i just kept growing and loving until finally admitting to myself, and over time other people, that i was a lady lover and always had been. it felt good to get the weight of the world off my chest and to be touching more chests.

i was living out and proud in my southern ass town and then bam, seizure. big yikes. so i had to stop. or maybe i didn't have to but that's what happened (what it felt like) i left my first big girl job and moved in with my parents in nashvegas, to then meet my wife long distance on bumble and ended up in tulsa.. we now live in chicago with our two cats, zucchini and quavo. a lot more has happened.. but i'll tell you about it. i'm just getting started.

# young wild and free

it's not your fault they never told you
the ropes that bound you were flimsy and
fraying
it's not your fault they told you
not to trust your own strength

they told you those things because
they knew when you broke free
they would lose you forever

the long silken locks they pinned you down to
grow
only served to tangle you up in the brush

they insisted you couldn't run
it wouldn't be natural
so you never tried

with pieces of your past self around you
the testament of your strength bound in your
hand
you'll never look back

# ya boring

men were almost interesting to me
that's why i dated them for so long
as a lesbian

heteronormativity is a bitch
and there are some men that truly are
almost interesting

there are lots of almost interesting people
and i put too much effort into those
that are almost, interesting

people i think i can make interesting
but they aren't
i'm breathing life into them
that's why they're dancing for me

you can make most people dance
if you know what motivates them
if you know what makes them dance
you can get them to

i hate how sinister that sounds
it's not like it doesn't take effort
it doesn't mean i get out unscathed
it takes my whole body

i've just learned the dance first
and i'm willing to drag you through rehearsal
until someone breaks down
or walks out

i've found a few gems that can just perform
there's no painful dance to learn
simply the singing of the music of my heart

with gleeful, euphoric, overwhelming
excitement
i ask them to join me on stage

# liar liar pants on fire

liar lying lies lies lies
spewing out of my mouth
sputtering
white hot and awkward

i don't even know why every word i said was
a lie
intentional or not it was all an illusion
but i only knew about half of it
and i had control over none of it

like a faucet of bs to fill in the gaps of a
personality
gushing hot garbage standing in for what wasn't
there

all i know now is
i only speak the truth
and it doesn't burn at all

# get the f*%n insta

i saw pictures of myself in situations
so fun
so cool
so insta worthy

and i'd zero in on me
sweaty
bulging
awkward
pained

and that's what i forced into the square but
it's not how i felt
or saw myself in my head
i mean only a little

no matter what the like count reflected
it felt like i was face to my face with the fact that
i couldn't be that happy

happy people have a glow
it comes at any shape or time
but you glow when body and soul are aligned
and mine looked rotten

i felt embarrassed to be there
like my presence interrupted the moment
i looked grotesque
and i don't know where to put that
when i'm just trying to live my life

cause i don't see myself that way
i'm fighting to see myself as funny

and goofy
and kind
and smart
and kinda cute
and worthy

life may imitate art, but it does not imitate
instagram

# so i'm the scariest thing in the lake

i crave to seek truth and define right from wrong
i want to rip off your sincerity like a bandaid
and inspect the scab that's left to ensure i
understand
allllll your intentions

my quest for justice will gnaw at your bones
as it liiiiterally always has mine
i'll take a hatchet to my memory and strip you
off slices
to prove i wasn't the lone culprit of my worst
acts

i don't mind looking bad, i've long known
that i'm the scariest thing in the lake
i'll drag you down amongst the bottom feeders
and show you how i do flips
if you're cool, we can play mermaids

# didn't need a dolla to make me holla

i turned myself out for no profit
i hated this thing
i wanted no part of this body
or the story that i had concocted for it

when i was 14 and 15 with no license
i'd meet them on the corner
and i don't know why

i said i was going on walks and i wasn't
i hated going for walks
i hated feeling like people were staring at me

they picked me up on the corner and we drove
up a hill
they already knew where to go or i told them
we usually did as much as i wanted
sometimes not

they'd drop me off close to the end of the street
and speed away
i felt nothing and didn't know why
they felt nothing but it seemed like they didn't
want to
i kept trying

i slept with a former teacher, but it wasn't
skeevy or anything
his pickup line was happy birthday when i
turned 18
and he'd always thought i was cute
since middle school

he rented a hotel for the first time
strictly car meet ups after that
until he once graciously let me come to his
house
that he lived in alone

later in college, i was touched by a shrimpy
blonde boy
while i wasn't conscious enough
to be touched at all

it's an experience that bonded my friend and i,
as he had done the same to her the year prior

and this is the body i have to live in
and i hate her
but she's all i've got

# sweet vs. sweat

the foul odor under a male
keeps you forcibly grounded in the present
grotesquely aware of the grime of life

overbearing thrusts seeking any and all openings
slap out a beat, marking the slowly elapsed
minutes
until the "high point" of ejaculation

the oppressive nature of receiving a man
in opposition to the transcendent experience of
embracing a woman
is almost unfathomable

seconds turn into hours of lazy, thorough
worshiping
i could be on another planet for all i know
what day is it again?

boobs are so cool

# huntsville hoe

(to the tune of.. idk just sing it)

huntsville ho, huntsville ho to the backseat she
will go
huntsville ho, huntsville ho to the backseat she
will go
she'll jerk you off and then she'll stop, just
kidding you're gunna blow

OH! huntsville ho, huntsville ho to the backseat
she will go
huntsville ho, huntsville ho to the backseat she
will go
you won't say hi, after she sucked you dry, when
you see her at little ro

HEY! huntsville ho, huntsville ho to the
backseat she will go
huntsville ho, huntsville ho to the backseat she
will go
you'll get to third base behind parkway place or
if she's classy bridgestreeeeet

OH! huntsville ho, huntsville ho to the backseat
she will go

huntsville ho if you can't get one, you'll get none
and end up wacking off alone... up on monte
sanoooo

# farmers market run in

"i ran into lana coin at the farmers market.
what were her sons names?
there was the older one, he was like.. the jock"

how do you tell your mom that "jock"
used to drive four hours through the night
because he had to see you
but he's never looked her in the eyes
never come over for dinner
how do you explain that?

how do you explain that he only ever picked you
up down the street,
never from the front door
that i outlasted girlfriends for eight years but as
what?

how can you explain to your mom
you were only ever a dirty secret
when you still don't get it

why did he get to decide i was only ever
dirty
a secret

i can't explain it to her
i can't explain it to me
so i didn't
i just named his other brothers

# two cheeseburger meal, plain, with a dr. pepper please

the decision to slip in and out of conventional
attractiveness
can be made at the drive through by ordering a
cheeseburger
chicken nuggets, fries, and a pie
yes i'll do the large

a few pounds on the scale from that supersize
and boys won't look at you at the bar
ten pounds being the difference between a
formal date
and a booty call

they'll always tap that but they won't always
talk about it
yikes that's a tough pill to swallow
i'll take the shot instead

i would have punched you in the face for a
medicine that slimmed my waist
but my wife likes my body wide, long, and tired
so the injection feels like a rejection
of the body i've come to know, love, and accept

but the world cheers
"thank god you finally care about yourself!
we had so many fears and we don't care you're
in tears
you're skinny!!" i've passed the ultimate test

# monsters inc

17

i keep waiting to say the magic words that make
you realize
i'm the worst

the key to unveiling the beast inside and you
finally see i'm gross
and filthy
and stinky

i'll say the thing that turns everyone away
has them running for the frickin hills

when you acquire the knowledge that i truly am
festering and rotten
creepy and twisted
weirdly vile

but i've waited a while and
no such luck
i keep spewing out daisies and sunshine
a few "fucks" but hey, i guess i am human

maybe it's not a monster under there
just a cute little girl in a leotard
spinning in circles

# a love letter to me

the only thing bound by law in my world; i live with an open heart, but i am its only keeper. i have the potential to invite someone in, let them inhabit me, take up space in my heart, all of it if they need. but i'll never give myself away. i am my only keeper. and i deserve to love myself fully and trust myself with my own happiness. i'll never give it away again.

i don't understand life without intimacy. so i'll continue to let people fill me up (take purchase in my soul? lol) some more than others. but i always have to be my number one priority. only then can i be all the other things.

i promise to myself that i will be my own biggest fan and i will choose myself, forsaking all others if it must be. it won't be. but if i'm living my full truth and i don't have a single soul still around, i wish myself the strength to walk away and be strong enough to rebuild. i think that would be rare, for it to be absolutely necessary to burn it all down to live true. but in those rare instances, i wish you all the strength in the world.

# just flicking the bean

before i was ready for porn
i would get on tinder and switch to girls

my heart would beat so fast the entire time
nervous someone would see my face
and i would have to explain

threesome

that was always going to be the excuse

but in the back of my mind i thought
it would make them caught too
so i hoped they wouldn't share my profile
either with confusion or curiosity
i knew i couldn't handle accusation or question

but i just wanted to see them
know that it was a reality for some people
people somewhere around me

i'd swipe through and see
mostly girls i didn't know
some i strained to know by association
just so it seemed more real

knowing without a doubt it was true
knowing they were doing what i wanted to be
doing
knowing they wanted it bad enough to just take
it

it was captivating
it was brave
it was arousing

and i'd touch myself to the thought of
other girls that wanted girls like i did
transfixed by the idea of the touch of a woman
to know that it wasn't made up

to fully embrace the truth that
i'd only ever felt truly myself in the company of
other women
i could only ever ebb and flow to the thought
and feel
of a woman

and as soon as the feeling crashed around me
i snapped like a rubberband

toggled back to the other side
shut the closet door
and forgot i was in there at all

# dishonor on you, dishonor on your cow

am i embarrassing generations around the
nation,
by talking about flicking the bean?

i strut out of the closet to the crowds' screams
"what do you mean on girls you're keen?"
"that is absolutely obscene!"

how can it be?
me just talking about my bean
brings distaste to everyone's face

oh, i know!
girls are so pretty in pearls and lace
it must be the fact
you can't keep up the pace

maybe it's not such a disgrace
and i shouldn't be erased
for talking about flicking her bean

i won't ever be a beauty queen
but you won't be able to demean
the fact that i just wanna talk about my
ding dang bean

# an ode to the middle school lesbians

maybe it was a deeper voice
a preference for boxy clothes
an awkwardness with men you just could not
shake
(they really are as awful as you thought, i am so
sorry)

but some tell gave you away
before you even really knew
even if you did know

you were clocked long before
you even had a chance to choose to hide it
no amount of boyfriends could stop the rumors

hopefully you got to tell the world
but if you didn't, i'm sorry
baby girl i am so sorry

the hiding, the not knowing, that was bad too
but i can't imagine the confusion of that
exposure
other people should not get to define you
i truly apologize that they did

if i did

just know you're so beautiful
so brave
so appreciated

you being yourself
you being authentic
you being pushed out early
helped a lot of people walk out late

# catch me on a good day

i might not have slept well last night
i might have some shit going on right now
you might have caught me on an off day
i'll give you that
but i promise you

there will come a day when you want to fuck me
and you will never
ever get to

# DND

25

i feel choked by your i love yous
used by your i miss yous
repulsed by your insistence to catch up

you don't want me
you use pleasantries to bind me
to a friendship we no longer have

# cool, theater girl

26

every time the people that love me look at me
with disdain
for dancing over my queso
doing cartwheels in the rain
singing in my broadway voice
cursing like a sailor
expressing my opinion

i die a little inside

but they're giving me a place to be
space to be weird and authentically myself
even if they tell me to stop

for some reason they always seem to need a
break from me
i hope i don't make them feel like that

# my storm girl

she loves storms
everything around them
and she is the storm that crashes with mine

the lightning of electric passion
the windy current of change and adaptation
the drenching purity of rain
the refreshing clarity after it all passes

i love her for all these reasons

but the electricity isn't what makes it
lightning strikes all the time
and the wind's change is unpredictable
it could knock you down or
simply blow a single strand of hair out of place

as much as i love my storm girl,
for the storm that rages in her,
that rages alongside the storm in me
i love her most for the way
she's learned to weather them

the way that being with her is the same as being
a kid

crammed in the bathroom with the people you
love most
waiting to see what's happened on the outside,
but knowing you have everything important in
front of you

she lives in the innermost part of my heart
with sturdy walls that stay sheltered from
everyday wear
and impenetrable from any front that could blow
through

she is my storm girl
and i'll love her as such

# 1-22-22 3:33

"yesss!!" she screamed emphatically "of course i
love you!" the need for understanding racing
through her pleading eyes. "do i need to get it
tattooed on my forehead? so you never forget?"
she asked earnestly.

and a week later she did
not on her forehead
but on her hand

a whimsical "h" from my own hand
that reminds her of me
and how magical life is when we enjoy the little
things

she came back home and placed her hand in
mine
and just said "look."
"look how much i love you forever
anyone will know anywhere
and you can never forget."

# noodles & sheila

i will get you the llama and i'll garden your
mind
i'll grind on you in the grocery store
and talk to you in a weird accent whenever

you make me so mad sometimes
and so deeply sad sometimes

i take so much pride in our relationship
and i ponder if i'm willing to die for it

i love you and you love me and that's not a
question
it's a statement of fact not opinion
i love you and you love me erin

i'm not sure what else to say
i'll see you when you get out of the bathroom
you mean the world to me

i wonder if we'll be together forever

i always decide i want to be

www.ingramcontent.com/pod-product-compliance
Lightning Source LLC
Chambersburg PA
CBHW071238140726
47996CB00007B/2661